NAPOLEON

THE STORY OF THE LITTLE CORPORAL

Bonaparte Crossing the Great Saint Bernard Pass, BY JACQUES-LOUIS DAVID.

 This painting is one of the most widely reprinted pictures of Napoleon, showing him heroically crossing the Alps on a prancing horse. The truth, however, is different. Napoleon actually crossed the mountains on a mule!

NAPOLEON

THE STORY OF THE LITTLE CORPORAL

By Robert Burleigh

Published in association with the American Federation of Arts

Abrams Books for Young Readers
New York

Portrait of Napoleon, First Consul, by Antoine-Jean Gros. *Napoleon Bonaparte in 1802. Only in his early thirties, Napoleon was already an acclaimed military genius and the First Consul of France. Gros has caught the penetrating gaze that captivated so many of Napoleon's contemporaries. His right hand touches a recently signed peace treaty, which gave France more power, more territory, and more prestige. This is one of the few portraits for which Napoleon posed from beginning to end.*

"You tell me it is impossible. There is no such word in French."

So said Napoleon Bonaparte, correcting a general who questioned one of his battle plans. Yet if any one word could sum up the life and career of Napoleon Bonaparte himself, that word would be *impossible*. Why? Well, no one would have guessed he was born to be a great general and Emperor of France!

He was born far from the nation's capital, Paris, on the small, remote island of Corsica near the coast of France. His family was not wealthy. Neither did Napoleon exhibit any special talents as a young child—his school record was only fair. He spoke French with a strange accent, and his spelling was terrible. As a young officer, his future in the army seemed unpromising, at best.

And yet—Napoleon became a general before age twenty-five and was famous as a military leader before age thirty. He became First Consul of France without having any political experience and reorganized French law and society in many ways.

Finally, as Emperor of France, he ruled over almost all of Western Europe. He led the world's largest army—up to that time—into Russia. He was even dethroned and exiled, yet regained his throne in less than a year.

Impossible?

Perhaps—but true!

"I never learned to laugh and play like the others."

The Bonapartes of Corsica were distantly connected to Italian nobility. But by the time Napoleon was born on August 15, 1769, that connection had long faded. Luckily for Napoleon, his father befriended the new rulers of Corsica, the French. Because of this, his son received a scholarship to a military school in France.

Napoleon's school days were not happy. He was a lonely student, often mocked by the wealthier cadets for his Corsican accent and his poverty. He was serious, but on the whole, average, in the classroom. His strongest subject was mathematics. But reading about the lives of great military leaders, such as Julius Caesar and Alexander the Great, moved him deeply. (He often liked to say, "History: Men should read nothing else.")

Despite his occasional difficulties at school, young Napoleon did show some signs of leadership. One story recounts how he led a group of other boys in a huge snowball fight. The story may be made up or exaggerated. But it probably comes from the fact that Napoleon had, in school and throughout his career, a deep interest in artillery—and in telling other people what to do!

When he graduated at the young age of sixteen, he became a lieutenant—but a lieutenant with a very uncertain future.

Left: **Napoleon as a Child with Mother**, by Denis Auguste Raffet. *In a picture made many years after the scene represented here, little Napoleon stands between an uncle and his mother. Napoleon's house on Corsica was not as richly furnished as the picture suggests. He remained very close to his beautiful and ambitious mother—known as "Madame mother"—all his life.*

Right: **Napoleon Being Snubbed by Other Cadets**, by Maurice Réalier-Dumas. *Poor and foreign-born, the young Napoleon was snubbed and taunted by other students (mostly sons of aristocrats) at military school. This was one reason for his early sympathy for the French Revolution.*

"My great talent
is that in everything I see clearly."

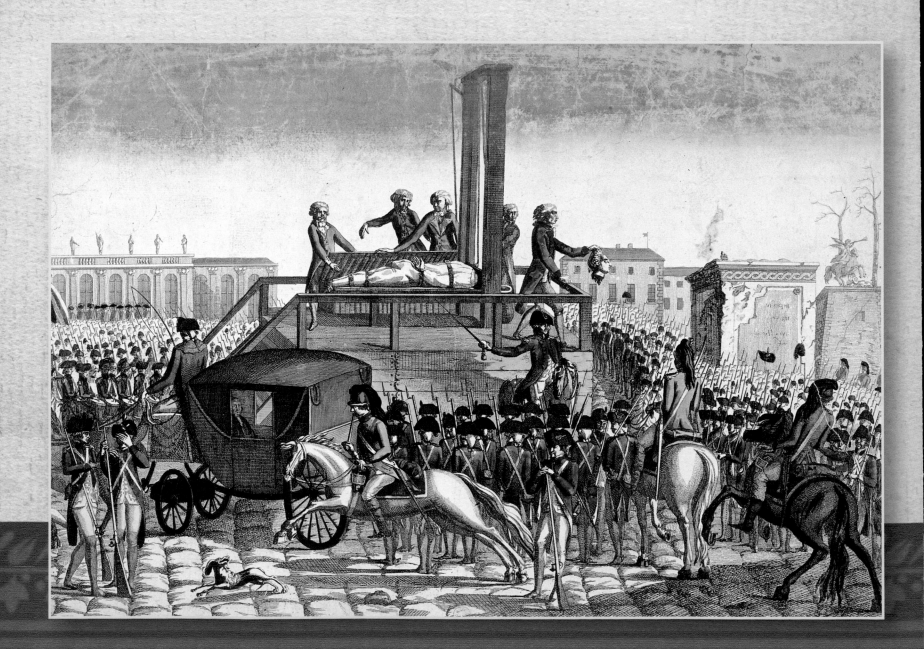

The French Revolution of 1789 changed France, Europe, and Napoleon's life in profound ways. The French people—heavily taxed, over-worked, and burdened by a rigid class system—rose up against their rulers.

The Revolution altered French society almost overnight. Under the slogan "Liberty, Equality, and Fraternity," a group of citizens—called Jacobins—soon took power. They greatly reduced the influence of the Catholic Church and took away the large estates owned by the very wealthy, then resold the lands. They also introduced voting rights, abolished slavery in French colonies, and even established a new calendar.

Some members of the ruling class, or nobility, fled. Others were tried in court and put to death. Even the king, Louis XVI, and his wife, Marie Antoinette, were sent to the guillotine during what is called the "Reign of Terror."

Napoleon never took part in these events. Instead, he waited and watched. He felt his time was coming. As to when or where, he still wasn't sure.

Above: **Protesters Invading Bastille**, BY UNKNOWN ARTIST. *The French Revolution erupted in 1789. Here the crowd breaks into the Bastille prison in Paris to free prisoners. The Revolution overthrew the ruling class that had been in power for centuries. By doing so, it opened up opportunities for newcomers to the scene—including Napoleon Bonaparte.*

Opposite page: **The Execution of Louis XVI**, BY UNKNOWN ARTIST. *In this grisly engraving, the executioner is holding King Louis XVI's head for the crowd to see. The king was one of several thousand people guillotined during the Reign of Terror in Paris. The execution of the king caused other European nations to declare war on France.*

 Siege of Toulon, BY PAUL GRÉGOIRE. *Napoleon's first military success came in 1793, when he used his*
knowledge of artillery to drive the English navy from a city on the French coast. He is shown here in the lower right,
peering through a spyglass. The French cannons, under his direction, are firing on English ships.

"I promised you brilliant successes!"

After the Revolution, as members of the nobility escaped or were killed, opportunities previously denied to the middle—and sometimes lower—classes opened up. In government, business, and the armed forces, members of these classes could now hope for positions of power.

Without the Revolution, Napoleon would likely have become no more than a lieutenant. In these times, however, anything was possible. Other European countries were opposed to revolutionary ideas. Some, such as Austria, tried to invade France. The French leaders organized their country to fight back. In the process, the French created the world's first "citizen army" (not made up exclusively of career soldiers).

In 1793, Lieutenant Bonaparte was sent to the seacoast town of Toulon, which was under attack by the British navy. Upon arriving, he quickly submitted a plan. Using his knowledge of artillery, he set up cannons at key points overlooking the harbor. The British fleet, attempting to bombard the city, was forced to retreat. Toulon remained under French control.

Never reluctant to boast, Napoleon immediately wrote to his superiors in Paris: "I promised you brilliant successes. And as you see, I have kept my word." His reward soon followed. He who had arrived a lieutenant soon found himself a brigadier general—at age twenty-four!

"In my youth I had illusions. I got rid of them fast."

Enthusiasm for the Revolution slowly waned. New leaders emerged. New governments formed. And always, each new government was in danger of being overthrown.

One such crisis took place in 1795. A large group of Royalists (those in favor of a king) attempted to take over the government offices. Napoleon—now General Bonaparte—was called upon to prevent the takeover.

His solution was simple—and bloody. He set up cannons in the street to fire on the marchers as they approached. Napoleon later called the brief cannon fire that followed, a "whiff of grapeshot." (*Grapeshot* was a word that described the small iron balls shot from a cannon, which together looked like a cluster of grapes.) The first shots came without warning. The next shots killed and wounded many. The government—for the moment—was secure.

Those in power now saw Napoleon as someone who would serve their interests. He was slowly becoming a significant figure in French politics. "Men," he had decided, "are moved by two levers only: self-interest and fear."

 Le 13 Vendemiaire, BY DENIS AUGUSTE RAFFET. *Napoleon looks on from his horse as cannon*
fire disperses a crowd of Parisian demonstrators. Shortly after defending the government, he was promoted again.
He was named Commander of the Army of the Interior.

"Sweet and matchless Josephine, how strangely you work upon my heart."

In 1795, Napoleon suddenly fell passionately in love. The woman was Rose de Beauharnais. History, however, knows her as Josephine, which in fact was the nickname given her by Napoleon. An older—and more cynical—Napoleon would say, "Love is a foolishness for two." At age twenty-six, though, he felt quite differently!

Josephine was a charming woman, attractive despite her darkly stained teeth, blackened from eating too much cane sugar. She had been married once before—to a nobleman who met his fate under the guillotine. (Josephine barely escaped the same fate herself.)

Both Napoleon and Josephine—mistakenly—believed the other was very rich. Their courtship was brief, and their honeymoon even briefer. Two days after their marriage, Napoleon left to assume command of the French army in Italy.

Yet from such unlikely beginnings, a kind of friendship developed. The couple's house on the outskirts of Paris was beautifully furnished (at a price: one historian states that Josephine cost France a million francs a year!). Over time the home became a place of calm and rest for the often war-weary husband.

Portrait Bust of the Empress Josephine, BY UNKNOWN ARTIST. *Napoleon's first wife, Josephine, was a party-loving beauty whose first husband had been guillotined. The youthful Napoleon fell deeply in love with her. Their marriage lasted for more than a dozen years.*

Left: **The Battle of Arcola,**
BY HORACE VERNET.
Napoleon leads his troops across a bridge.
This occurred during his first campaign as
Commander-in-Chief in northern Italy.
He was twice surrounded by the enemy, and
several horses were shot out from under
him. This picture, like all those showing
Napoleon at war, was done after the fact.

Right: **French Army Crossing the**
Alps, BY CHARLES MULLER. *Napoleon's*
second Italian campaign was another major
triumph. In it, he surprised the enemy in
northern Italy by crossing a part of the Alps.
The dangerous crossing caused people to
compare Napoleon to the ancient general
Hannibal, who 2,000 years earlier had led
his army over the Alps to battle the Romans.

"From that moment, I saw what I might be."

Napoleon's first full-scale command of an army—in northern Italy—made his reputation as a brilliant general. He rapidly established his authority among other officers, who at first doubted his ability to lead. He was quick to size up the battlefield and quick to move his soldiers to precisely determined spots. Soon he had the French army on the attack. Napoleon liked to say, "The worst thing in any venture is indecision."

He won the loyalty of his troops, too. Loading cannons side-by-side with low-ranking soldiers, Napoleon earned the nickname of the Little Corporal. On another occasion, he led his men across a key bridge. It was at this moment, he later said, that he had the first inkling of his destiny.

The 1796 Italian campaign made him a celebrity in France. A few years later, he led another large army over the Alps in what was then thought to be an impossible ascent. The result? Another victory in Italy and even more praise from his country!

Napoleon's success in Italy brought more than prestige to France. The conquering general sent gold, silver, and even artworks back to Paris. (Some of these artworks—by Leonardo da Vinci, among others—helped found the now-famous Louvre Museum.) If anyone protested his looting of Italian art, Napoleon had a curt reply: "All men of genius," he declared, "are French!"

"The time I passed in Egypt was the most beautiful of my life."

In the minds of most Europeans, Egypt was filled with wonder and mystery. And it was no different for Napoleon. Assigned to invade England in 1798, Napoleon soon thought the better of it. Instead—ever the adventurer—he suggested leading troops into Egypt. His plan was to block England's trade route to India.

Napoleon sailed with 50,000 soldiers to the Egyptian coast. He also brought along many scientists, whose job it was to study the Middle East. The expedition began well. Because the French army possessed the most advanced weapons in the world, it easily defeated the sword-brandishing army of Egyptian Mamelukes in what came to be called the "Battle of the Pyramids."

"Soldiers," Napoleon proclaimed, "from the summit of yonder pyramids, forty centuries look down upon you!"

Then things took a turn for the worse. The British navy surprised the French fleet at anchor and destroyed it. The French army was trapped in Egypt. The scientists, for their part, continued making many discoveries. (One was the Rosetta Stone, which was later used to translate ancient Egyptian hieroglyphics.) The army, on the other hand, suffered from defeats and sickness.

And Napoleon? Before the bitter end, he sailed secretly back to France, where he was given a hero's welcome. (The bad news hadn't arrived yet.) Egyptian obelisks and sphinx fountains be-

came the rage in Paris. "Great reputations are made only in the East," Napoleon liked to say. And in his case, at least, it was true. For years, Napoleon's name and part of his fame would be linked to an Egypt that he had never won!

Battle of the Pyramids, July 21, 1798, BY FRANÇOIS GEORGIN. *Nothing added to Napoleon's fame more than his expedition to Egypt. In the Battle of the Pyramids, Napoleon's modern army easily defeated the Mamelukes (rulers of Egypt). Napoleon, it is said, even considered converting to Islam.*

"I love power as a musician loves his violin."

Napoleon was young, ambitious, eloquent, and handsome. (Was he also short? Yes and no. He was only a few inches over five feet tall, but this was just slightly below the average height of a man of his time.)

What people especially noted about him were his piercing eyes. All who met him commented on the gray-blue gaze that seemed to suggest hidden depths. One awestruck German poet wrote, "On his face was written: you shall have no other god but me!" In person, he commanded respect. He also commanded the entire French army.

When Napoleon returned from Egypt, France was in turmoil. People wanted, above all else, a stable government. Some politicians—mostly rich men—linked their futures with Napoleon's. In November 1799, Napoleon and two others seized power. They took their new titles from old Roman ones—Consuls. Napoleon, for his part, became the *First* Consul. His political life was about to start.

What did the French people think? A vote held in 1800 was overwhelmingly in Napoleon's favor. Three million voted for the new government, while only 1,500 voted no! The Little Corporal was suddenly the most powerful man in France.

 Opposite page: **Installation of the Conseil d'Etat at the Palais du Petit-Luxembourg on December 25, 1799,** BY LOUIS-CHARLES-AUGUSTE COUDER. *In the rough-and-tumble world of French politics, Napoleon (the center figure in the top right) became one of three consuls, who in effect ruled the country. At the time of this painting, First Consul Napoleon was just thirty years old.*

I am the state—I alone am here the representative of the people."

Napoleon had supreme confidence in his own ideas. He thought he knew what France needed—and what French citizens wanted. Without delay, he went to work.

Throughout the country, different regions had different laws. What was legal in one city might be illegal in another! Napoleon soon changed that. In fact, his legal system, the *Code Napoléon*, is still in place in France. He set up a national bank to help the economy through hard times. He established a Legion of Honor to reward French soldiers and private citizens. He expanded education. He even healed the rift between France and the Catholic Church, while also encouraging religious tolerance.

Napoleon was personally involved in overseeing many of these changes. His curiosity and knowledge were wide-ranging. He sometimes worked eighteen hours a day, barely slowing down to eat (fifteen minutes was his usual stay at the table). His capacity for keeping facts at his fingertips was amazing, too. He often dictated several letters—to several waiting secretaries—at the same time! There was good reason why the bee—that busy insect—was made a Napoleonic insignia, or symbol.

He installed a constitution (a set of laws), too, even though he had doubts about democracy, self-government, and the people's right to choose. "A constitution should be short," he once quipped, "and obscure."

 Assassination Attempt, BY JOB. *There were several attempts on Napoleon's life. In 1800, his carriage narrowly missed being blown up by an assassin's bomb. He and Josephine escaped, but the blast killed more than twenty people.*

"If only our father could see us now!"

These, it is said, were the words Napoleon whispered into his brother's ear. The place was Paris. The date was December 2, 1804. And the event? Napoleon's coronation as Emperor of France! Napoleon had long worried about keeping his power. Indeed, there had been several attempts on his life. Royalists hoped to bring back the family of the late king. By becoming Emperor—once again approved by a vote—Napoleon further entrenched himself as the rightful ruler.

The coronation ceremony was a spectacular event, planned to the tiniest detail. The Pope even came from Rome. The clothes and royal costumes were lavish, ushering in a new era of pomp and high fashion. To top it all off, Napoleon crowned himself, setting the crown on his own head! Next he proceeded to crown the Empress, Josephine.

In declaring France an empire—and thus no longer a republic—Napoleon did not please everyone. Throughout Europe, many who had sympathized with the French Revolution felt Napoleon had betrayed it. The composer Ludwig van Beethoven was about to dedicate his Third Symphony to Napoleon. Hearing of the coronation, however, Beethoven tore up the dedication page in disgust!

Coronation of Emperor Napoleon and Josephine at Notre-Dame on December 2, 1804, BY JACQUES-LOUIS DAVID. *Having first crowned himself Emperor, Napoleon places a crown on the Empress Josephine. This huge painting (the participants were shown life-size!) took several years to finish and was partly directed by suggestions from Napoleon.*

"Soldiers generally win battles; generals generally get credit for them."

Napoleon made sure *he* got credit for his army's victories. In his many bulletins to the home front, he consistently put himself in the best light. Napoleon was—as one historian jests—"his own best press agent."

The 1805 Battle of Austerlitz was his greatest military triumph. Napoleon hid a large number of his troops in a mist-shrouded ravine. When the enemy drew close, the French stormed forth and drove out the combined armies of Austria and Russia.

Napoleon's special tactic was to detect the weak spot in the enemy's front line—and, with great speed and a mass of quickly concentrated troops, to attack at that point. He could then turn and defeat one part of the enemy's army, and then the other. "The side which stays behind its fortified lines is always defeated," he wrote.

Another writer summed up Napoleon's military philosophy this way: "He wanted to win; they—his opponents—merely wanted not to lose." He may have been affectionately called the Little Corporal, but to most military historians, he has long been considered one of the greatest generals in human history.

Opposite page: **Napoleon's Camp on the Eve of the Battle of Austerlitz, December 1, 1805,** BY LOUIS-FRANÇOIS LEJEUNE. *The evening before one of his most important victories (the Battle of Austerlitz, 1805), Napoleon made surprise visits to many outposts. Wherever he went, soldiers lit torches and small fires, lighting up the entire plain.*

Above: **The Plumb Pudding in Danger**, BY JAMES GILLRAY.
*The Napoleonic period was a great age of newspaper cartoons. Here an
English artist shows Napoleon, on the right, carving up the world with
his British enemy to decide who would get what "serving," or territory.
Before and during Napoleon's reign, France and England were at war
for more than twenty years.*

Right: **Street Crier**, BY UNKNOWN ARTIST. *News from the
battlefront was often shown on prints put up in public squares
throughout France. Street criers added to the drama by shouting out
details of the events. In this scene, the poster and the street crier are
announcing, "Peace, thanks to the immortal Napoleon."*

"Wherever wood can swim, there I am sure to find the flag of England."

By 1807, after more victorious battles, France was supreme in western Europe. French borders had expanded. Austria had been humbled. Prussia had been defeated. Russia had retreated eastward. Several smaller states had been created—often ruled by Napoleon's siblings! These smaller states looked to Paris for their orders.

Yet one nation did not bow to Napoleon. Britain, behind the "wooden walls" of its powerful navy, remained hostile. At the Battle of Trafalgar (off the coast of Spain, 1805), the English dealt a deadly blow to the French fleet. True, the English had as yet no armed forces on the continent, but their country was safe from invasion. England was also rich enough (due to its overseas trade) to finance uprisings against France wherever possible.

Napoleon hoped to punish "perfidious Albion" (Albion is a literary name for Britain). He declared a continental blockade. No British ship could trade at any European port. The plan worked—for a while. But in the end, it only caused those of Napoleon's subject states that could not get goods from other parts of the world to grow restless. When the time came, they would be ready to revolt.

"Too much power ends by depraving even the most honest man."

Napoleon's ambition to extend his power never ceased. In 1808 he attempted to place one of his brothers on the throne of Spain. Napoleon believed Spain was a weak, backward country that would welcome the French. He was soon surprised.

When the French army entered Spain, the Spanish people fought back. Against French guns, the Spaniards often used homemade weapons. This spontaneous uprising gave the world the phrase "guerilla war." (*Guerilla* means "little war" in Spanish.) Napoleon was forced to use a large number of French troops in a struggle that drained France and lasted for years.

At home, his absolute power created another kind of tyranny. Although Napoleon was not a particularly cruel man, he kept a tight rein on French political life.

He prided himself on promoting soldiers and civilians without regard to their wealth or social class. At the same time, he imprisoned or exiled political opponents, censored plays, and closed many newspapers. "Newspapers," he stated bluntly, "should be confined to advertising."

Above: **Joachim Murat, King of Naples, Brother-in-Law of Napoleon**, BY A. GALLIANO. *Napoleon liked to promote soldiers because of their skill and bravery, rather than their wealth or social status. Joachim Murat was a famous marshall (high-level general) who rose through the ranks.*

Opposite page: **Third of May, 1808**, BY FRANCISCO DE GOYA, 1814. *French soldiers execute Spanish patriots in Madrid in 1808. Napoleon expected to invade and easily conquer Spain. Instead, the Spanish people revolted against the invaders.*

Left: **Napoleon II, Duke of Reichstadt**, by Moritz Michael Daffinger. *Napoleon's son François-Charles-Joseph Bonaparte (known as Napoleon II) was placed under the watchful eye of his grandfather, Emperor Franz I, in Vienna, Austria. After Napoleon was first exiled (1814), the young boy would never see his father again.*

Right: **Portrait of Empress Marie-Louise, Second wife of Napoleon I, Daughter of Emperor Franz I of Austria**, by François Gérard. *Marie-Louise, Napoleon's second wife and daughter of the Emperor of Austria, had been brought up to believe Napoleon was an evil man. She seems, though, to have truly fallen in love with her new husband. But she, too, along with her young son, was forced to return to her father's house when Napoleon was exiled.*

"I am an upstart soldier."

Napoleon never forgot that his rule rested on shaky grounds. "I am an upstart soldier," he once said. "The day when I cease to be strong and therefore feared—I will not survive."

For a long time he hoped that he and Josephine might have a son. A son, in Napoleon's mind, would give the Bonaparte line a permanent place in France. Finally, when no son (or any child) was born, he decided to divorce his wife of many years. A print of the period shows Josephine on her knees pleading while Napoleon looks on with a sad face. But the deed was done.

Napoleon first proposed to the Russian czar's sister—and was turned down. Next, he turned to the Austrian emperor's daughter. This proposal was accepted. Marie-Louise and Napoleon were married on April 2, 1810. Although it was only an arranged marriage, letters from the young wife indicate she soon fell in love with her "captivating" husband.

To Napoleon's great delight, a son was born a year later. The emperor doted on the infant. However, the glory that Napoleon foresaw for his son was not to be. François-Charles-Joseph Bonaparte, King of Rome (the name and title given to the new child), never ruled France—or Rome, either.

After Moscow, *fortune ceased to smile on me.*"

One European nation (besides England) still remained outside Napoleon's control. This was Russia, a country, in Napoleon's words, "way at the back of beyond." When the Russian czar defied Napoleon by trading with England, the French made plans to attack.

The army that invaded Russia in 1812 was the largest in world history up to that time: around 450,000 men. Napoleon crossed into Russia hoping to defeat the Russians in one decisive battle. Yet such a battle never took place. The Russians retreated, deeper and deeper into their country. They also destroyed goods, food, and grain behind them. The invaders, therefore, could not "live off the land."

"I should have stayed two weeks," Napoleon later wrote. Instead, perhaps dreaming of the ancient conquests of such generals as Julius Caesar, he pressed ahead. It was a fatal mistake.

The French reached Moscow, the Russian capital, only to find it burning to the ground. Winter descended. Too late, Napoleon tried to pull back. The withdrawal became a frantic retreat. Tens of thousands of soldiers (along with 80,000 horses!) died from cold, starvation, or guerilla attacks. Even the emperor barely escaped capture. The army dwindled to a ragtag band of about 40,000. It was one of the most crushing reversals in military history. For Napoleon it was the beginning of the end.

Left: The Fire of Moscow in 1812, BY UNKNOWN ARTIST. *A woodcut shows Moscow ablaze in 1812 as the French reach the city. Rather than fight the French army head-on, the Russians retreated into their vast countryside. The French found nothing but smoldering farms and burning cities. When winter arrived, Napoleon was forced to retreat.*

Right: From Top to Bottom, BY UNKNOWN ARTIST. *A contemporary cartoon shows an awkwardly balanced Napoleon trying to stretch his power from Spain to Russia. The tumbling hat and scepter remind the viewer that it can't be done!*

The Farewell of Napoleon I to the Imperial Guard in the Courtyard of the White Horse at Fontainebleau, April 20,
1814, BY HORACE VERNET AND ALPHONSE ANTOINE MONTFORT. *"Once more, good-bye to you, my old comrades."*
Napoleon, forced to give up his throne and leave France, bids a tearful farewell to many of the generals who had served under
him for nearly twenty years. It was April 20, 1814. Napoleon was exiled to Elba, a small island off the coast of Italy.

"The bullet that will kill me is not yet cast."

Encouraged by Napoleon's defeat in Russia, other European nations joined in the attack. A new coalition (a coalition is a group of cooperating nations) including Russia, Prussia, and Austria marched toward French soil. Napoleon was now on the defensive. He fought back brilliantly, winning a number of isolated battles. But his army was outnumbered. Slowly, the coalition advanced on Paris.

The allies offered Napoleon a truce—on the condition that France return to its old borders. He refused, still hoping for a miraculous turn in his fortunes. When none came, a treaty was signed on April 11, 1814. Napoleon's wife and young son were whisked off to Austria. Napoleon himself was forced into exile, under English guard, and Louis XVIII assumed the throne of France.

The place chosen for Napoleon's (first) exile was an island not far from Corsica: Elba. He was promised money and a small band of soldiers. "I shall not need anything," he declared. "A soldier does not need much space to die in."

Had Napoleon accepted his fate? It might seem so. But the story was not yet over.

"Shoot your emperor, if you wish!"

On Elba, bored, restless, and ever-ambitious, Napoleon bided his time. He saw that many French people were not happy under the new king. With a small band of soldiers, he slipped past his English guards and sailed for the south of France. It was the start of what historians call the Hundred Days.

Marching north, Napoleon was greeted with enthusiasm. Louis XVIII sent troops to arrest or shoot the former emperor. Napoleon challenged the soldiers, who lowered their rifles and rushed to the former leader's side. The king fled. By the time Napoleon reached Paris, he was once again ruler of France!

He now tried to win over his many critics. He changed the constitution, giving more freedom to French citizens. Yet was it enough? The European allies once more prepared to attack.

The final battle of the Napoleonic Wars took place in Belgium on June 18, 1815. Here, near the town of Waterloo, Napoleon's army faced a combination of English and Prussian troops. "All great events," he would later say, "hang by a single thread." For Napoleon, on this day, the thread snapped.

He made a careful plan. He hoped to move quickly and deal with each opposing army separately. It never happened. The English and the Prussians were able to join forces. In a dreadful battle—in which one in four of all soldiers

were killed or wounded—the French army was defeated. Napoleon (who had prepared for possible
defeat and escape by sewing diamonds into the
upholstery of his carriage) raced back to Paris.

What now?

Where to?

The Day after Waterloo, ENGRAVED BY MATTHEW
DUBOURG AFTER JOHN HEAVISIDE CLARKE. *A scene after the
great battle of Waterloo, June 18, 1815. In all, 40,000 soldiers
(one in four of all combatants) were killed or wounded. The English
army, under the command of the Duke of Wellington, along with the
Prussians, defeated the smaller French army.*

"Whatever shall we do in this remote spot? Well, we shall write our memoirs."

Napoleon's second exile was far harsher than his first. Fearful of another escape, the European allies shipped their onetime adversary to a bleak, windswept island in the South Atlantic. St. Helena was an English possession, but it was far from Europe and far from the African coast.

Napoleon was given a house, a garden, and freedom to roam the island. Briefly, he dreamed of returning to his homeland. More and more, however, he mulled over his days of triumph and glory by dictating his memoirs in great detail. In his mind, he relived winning battles and refought losing ones, searching for the reasons why. When these memoirs became available in France, some became "bestsellers."

The days dragged by. Forgotten by his second wife (Josephine had died earlier) and his young son, Napoleon's spirits sank. Melancholy overtook the once active soldier and statesman. He left the house less and less. He became ill. Finally, surrounded by a few remaining followers, he died on May 5, 1821—at age fifty-one.

His last words were "Chief of the Army . . . Josephine."

Above: **Napoleon I Dictating His Notes to His Young Assistant on Ile Ste. Helene**, BY UNKNOWN ARTIST. *During his final years, on St. Helena, Napoleon dictated his political testament and his memoirs. With their publication, the Napoleonic legend was born. He claimed that all he did over the years was for the love of France. He remained a prisoner on St. Helena from 1815 until his death in 1821.*

Opposite page: **Napoleon on Board the Bellerophon**, BY WILLIAM QUILLER ORCHARDSON. *Napoleon hoped to spend the days of his second exile in England. Here, aboard the British ship* Bellerophon, *he takes his last look at the French coast. His final destination, however, would not be England but St. Helena, a small, barren island in the South Atlantic.*

"There is no immortality but the memory that is left in the minds of men."

Some memories fade; others grow brighter with time. Had hundreds of thousands of Frenchmen died or been wounded in almost two decades of war? Had many more Europeans—soldiers and civilians—perished in the carnage? Had France fallen under the tyrannical rule of one man?

For some, these facts became blurred. They dimmed against the memory of the man who, at least in his own estimation, had done everything "for love of France." Napoleon presented himself as both a man of war and a man of peace. He also claimed to have protected the ideals of the French Revolution. "Every Frenchman could say

in my reign—I shall be minister, duke, baron, if I earn it—even king."

The story of Napoleon grew larger than life. He came to stand for the hero who, starting with almost nothing, had nearly conquered the world. The Napoleonic "legend," in the words of one observer, became "his lasting conquest."

"What a romance my life has been," Napoleon boasted. And many agreed.

"An extraordinary man," said a statesman who knew Napoleon well. "His career is the most outstanding that has occurred in one thousand years!" In 1840, Napoleon's remains were taken

from St. Helena to an ornate crypt in Paris in Les Invalides, a former veterans' hospital. There the legend lives on—as tens of thousands of people each year still visit the final resting place of the man his loyal soldiers called the Little Corporal: Napoleon Bonaparte.

Napoleon's Tomb. *Napoleon was buried on St. Helena. In 1840, however, his remains were taken to France. They were placed in Les Invalides, in Paris, where they still lie in a large tomb, surrounded by reminders of his great victories.*

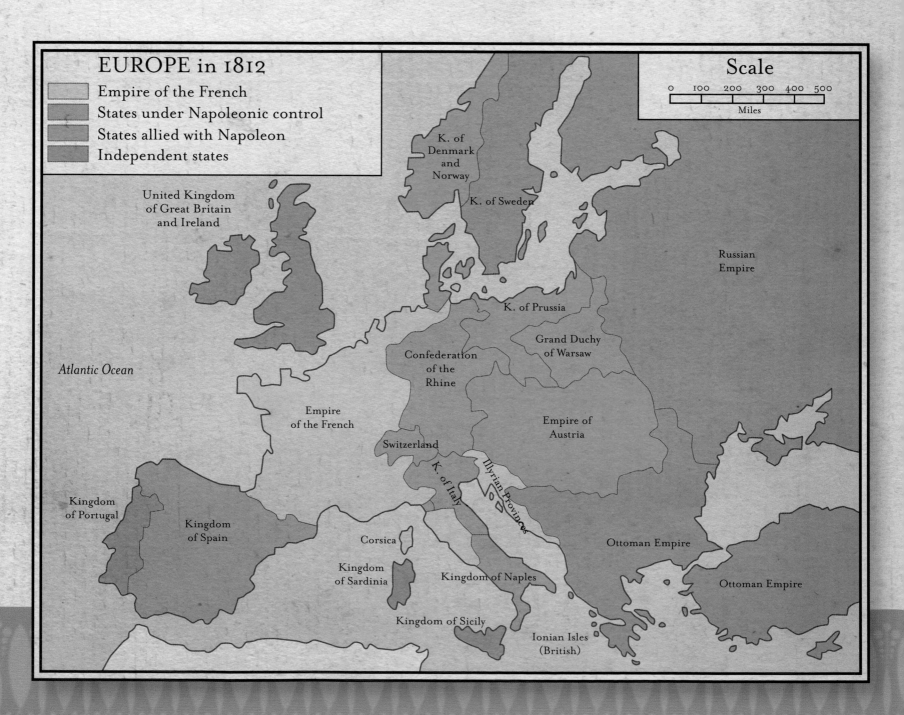

EUROPE in 1812

Empire of the French
States under Napoleonic control
States allied with Napoleon
Independent states

Scale

0 100 200 300 400 500
Miles

United Kingdom
of Great Britain
and Ireland

K. of
Denmark
and
Norway

K. of Sweden

Russian
Empire

Atlantic Ocean

K. of Prussia

Grand Duchy
of Warsaw

Confederation
of the
Rhine

Empire
of the French

Empire of
Austria

Switzerland

K. of Italy

Illyrian Provinces

Kingdom
of Portugal

Kingdom
of Spain

Corsica

Ottoman Empire

Kingdom
of Sardinia

Kingdom of Naples

Ottoman Empire

Kingdom of Sicily

Ionian Isles
(British)

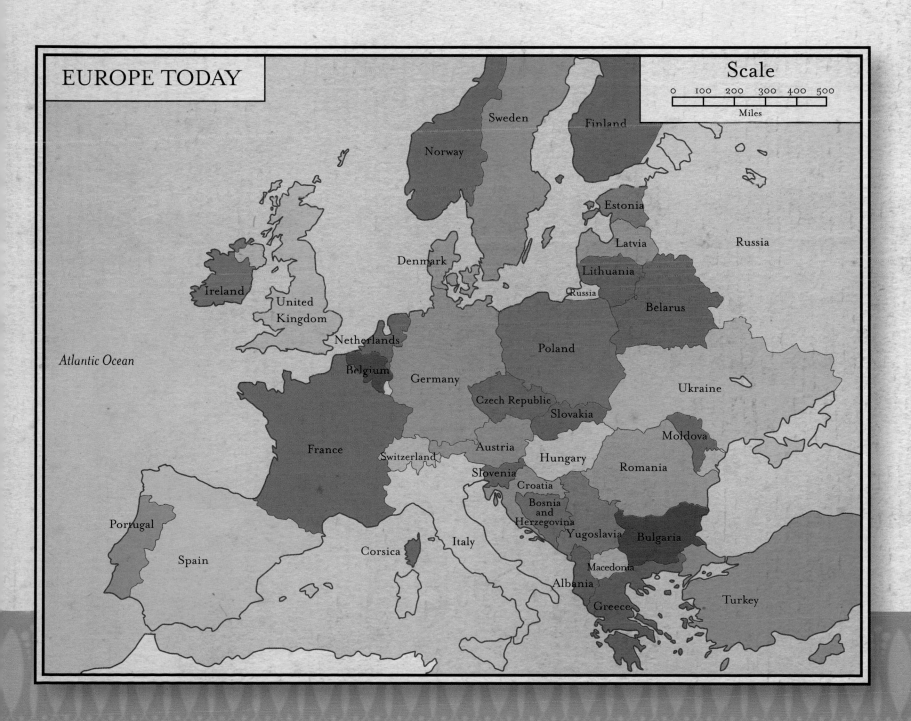

EUROPE TODAY

Scale

0   100   200   300   400   500

Miles

Sweden

Finland

Norway

Estonia

Russia

Latvia

Denmark

Lithuania

Russia

Belarus

Ireland

United
Kingdom

Netherlands

Poland

Belgium

Atlantic Ocean

Germany

Czech Republic

Ukraine

Slovakia

Austria

Moldova

France

Switzerland

Hungary

Romania

Slovenia

Croatia

Portugal

Bosnia
and
Herzegovina

Yugoslavia

Bulgaria

Spain

Corsica

Italy

Macedonia

Albania

Greece

Turkey

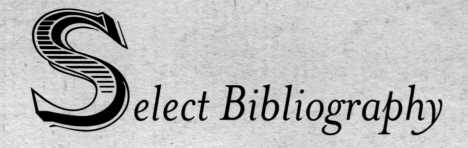

Select Bibliography

Chandler, David G. *The Illustrated Napoleon*. New York: Henry Holt and Company, 1990.

Covington, Richard. "Napoleon Bonaparte." *U.S. News and World Report: The Great Conquerors* (January 2006): pp. 64–69.

Durant, Will and Ariel. *The Age of Napoleon*. New York: Simon and Schuster, 1975.

Englund, Steven. *Napoleon: A Political Life*. New York: Scribner, 2004.

Gray, Daniel S. *In the Words of Napoleon*. Troy, Alabama: Troy State University Press, 1977.

Herold, J. Christopher. *The Horizon Book of the Age of Napoleon*. New York: American Heritage Publishing Company, 1983.

Horne, Alistair. *The Age of Napoleon*. New York: The Modern Library, 2004.

Johnson, Paul. *Napoleon*. New York: Penguin Putnam, Inc., 2002.

Markham, Felix. *Napoleon*. New York: Penguin Group (USA) Inc., 1966.

Mondadoni, Arnoldo, ed. *The Life and Times of Napoleon*. Philadelphia—New York: Curtis Publishing Company, 1966.

Wilson-Smith, Timothy. *Napoleon: Man of War, Man of Peace*. New York: Carroll & Graf Publishers, 2002.

In addition, I have also used two anthologies for some of the primary quotations found in the text:

Kaplan, Justin, gen. ed. *Bartlett's Familiar Quotations (Sixteenth Edition)*. Boston: Little, Brown and Company, 1992.

Miner, Margaret, and Hugh Rawson, eds. *The New International Dictionary of Quotations (Second Edition)*. New York: The Penguin Group, 1994.

Below are the sources for the quotations from Napoleon that introduce each section. See the bibliography for the full citations.

Page 5: *Bartlett's*, p. 370
Page 6: Englund, p. 20
Page 8: Englund, p. 59
Page 11: Markham, p. 26
Page 12: Herold, p. 28
Page 14: Horne, p. 55
Page 17: Horne, p. 8
Page 18: Englund, p. 136
Page 21: Covington, p. 67
Page 22: *New International Dictionary*, p. 442
Page 24: Markham, p. 113
Page 27: *New International Dictionary*, p. 245
Page 29: *Bartlett's*, p. 371
Page 30: Chandler, p. 162
Page 33: Wilson-Smith, p. 75
Page 34: Englund, p. 378
Page 37: *New International Dictionary*, p. 386
Page 39: Markham, p. 226
Page 40: *Bartlett's*, p. 370
Page 42: Herold, p. 407

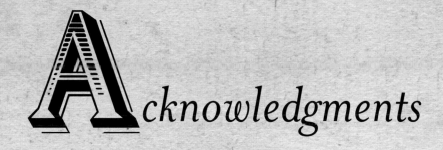

Acknowledgments

The first people I must thank are the many writers and scholars whose work has helped me understand the complex and contradictory subject that is Napoleon Bonaparte. The bibliography lists most of the sources used, though I have picked up an anecdote here or a fact there by skimming in various other places.

A special appreciation goes out to the staff at Abrams Books for Young Readers, in particular editor Howard Reeves, editorial assistant Maggie Lehrman, and designer Celina Carvalho, for their hard work and efforts to ensure that the book be as good as it can be. I also want to thank the people at the American Federation of Arts for obtaining and clearing rights for the artwork as well as offering valuable criticism. This includes Alec Spangler, Sarah Ingber, and especially Michaelyn Mitchell.

And as usual, my heartfelt thanks goes out to my always supportive wife, Jenny Roberts.

Author's note

One of the pleasures—yes, pleasures!—of researching the subject of Napoleon is that there are so many Napoleons. There is a reason more than 600,000 books and articles have been written about him since his death more than 180 years ago. So many years—and historians are still debating some basic questions: Was he the protector of the ideals of the French Revolution—a true French patriot? Or was he all cold, calculating ambition? Was his career merely an example of being at the right place at the right time? Or was he the type of genius who rarely appears on the world scene?

This small book can hardly answer these questions. Rather, I hope it briefly captures the broad outlines and drama of a special life, one that dazzled his contemporaries and still fires the imagination of the present time. I have drawn on Napoleon's own words to anchor each section, hoping this will give readers a sense of his complex personality. He was a man of action—of that there is no doubt. But he was also a man of words—witty, insightful, and ready to comment on anything and everything—his own life most of all!

ILLUSTRATION CREDITS

Cover, p. 2 Jacques-Louis David, *Bonaparte Crossing the Great Saint Bernard Pass*, 1801. Châteaux de Malmaison et Bois-Préau, Rueil-Malmaison. Photo: Erich Lessing / Art Resource, NY **Back cover, spine, p. 26** Louis-François Lejeune, *Napoleon's Camp on the Eve of the Battle of Austerlitz, December 1, 1805* (detail), 1808. Châteaux de Versailles et de Trianon, Versailles. Photo: RMN-G/J. Schormans; Réunion des Musées Nationaux / Art Resource, NY **p. 4** Antoine-Jean Gros, *Portrait of Napoleon, First Consul*. Musée National de la Légion d'Honneur, Paris. Photo: Réunion des Musées Nationaux / Art Resource, NY **p. 7 top** Denis Auguste Raffet, *Napoleon as a Child with Mother* **p. 7 bottom** Maurice Réalier-Dumas, *Napoleon Being Snubbed by Other Cadets*, 1906. Anne S. K. Brown Military Collection, Brown University Library **p. 8** Unknown artist, *The Execution of Louis XVI*. Musée de la Ville de Paris, Musée Carnavalet, Paris. Photo: Erich Lessing / Art Resource, NY **p. 9** Unknown artist, *Protesters Invading Bastille*, 1789. **p. 10** Paul Grégoire, *Siege of Toulon*. Bibliothèque nationale de France **p. 13** Denis Auguste Raffet, *Le 13 Vendemiaire*. **p. 15** Unknown artist, *Portrait Bust of the Empress Josephine*, 1807–09. Châteaux de Malmaison et Bois-Préau, Rueil-Malmaison. Photo: Réunion des Musées Nationaux / Art Resource, NY **p. 16 top** Horace Vernet, *The Battle of Arcola*. Anne S. K. Brown Military Collection, Brown University Library **p. 16 bottom** Charles Muller, *French Army Crossing the Alps*, n.d. Anne S. K. Brown Military Collection, Brown University Library **p. 19** François Georgin, *Battle of the Pyramids, July 21, 1798*. Musée de la Ville de Paris, Musée Carnavalet, Paris. Archives Charmet / The Bridgeman Art Library **p. 20** Louis-Charles-Auguste Couder, *Installation of the Conseil d'Etat at the Palais du Petit-Luxembourg on December 25, 1799*, 1856. Conseil d'Etat. Photo: Herve Lewandowski; Réunion des Musées Nationaux / Art Resource, NY **p. 23** Job, *Assassination Attempt*, 1921. Anne S. K. Brown Military Collection, Brown University Library **p. 25** Jacques-Louis David, *Coronation of Emperor Napoleon and Josephine at Notre-Dame on December 2, 1804*, 1806–07. Louvre, Paris (3699). Photo: Réunion des Musées Nationaux / Art Resource, NY **p. 28 left** James Gillray, *The Plumb Pudding in Danger*, 1805. Private collection. Photo: The Bridgeman Art Library **p. 28 right** Unknown artist, *Street Crier*. Hennin collection. **p. 30** Francisco de Goya, *Third of May, 1808*, 1814. Museo del Prado, Madrid. Photo: Scala / Art Resource, NY **p. 31** A. Galliano, *Joachim Murat, King of Naples, Brother-in-Law of Napoleon*, 1813. Palazzo Reale, Caserta, Italy. Photo: Alfredo Dagli Orti; Bildarchiv Preussischer Kulturbesitz / Art Resource, NY **p. 32 left** Moritz Michael Daffinger, *Napoleon II, Duke of Reichstadt*. Musée Condé, Chantilly. Photo: R.G. Ojeda; Réunion des Musées Nationaux / Art Resource, NY **p. 32 right** François Gérard, *Portrait of Empress Marie-Louise, Second Wife of Napoleon I, Daughter of Emperor Franz I of Austria*. Louvre, Paris. Photo: Erich Lessing / Art Resource, NY **p. 35 top** Unknown artist, *The Fire of Moscow in 1812*, ca. 1812. Color engraving. Kunstbibliothek, Staatliche Museen zu Berlin. Photo: Knud Petersen; Bildarchiv Preussischer Kulturbesitz / Art Resource, NY **p. 35 bottom** Unknown artist, *From Top to Bottom*, 1812. Anne S. K. Brown Military Collection, Brown University Library **p. 36** Horace Vernet and Alphonse Antoine Montfort, *The Farewell of Napoleon I to the Imperial Guard in the Courtyard of the White Horse at Fontainebleau, April 20, 1814*. Châteaux de Versailles et de Trianon, Versailles. Photo: Gerard Blot; Réunion des Musées Nationaux / Art Resource, NY **p. 39** Engraved by Matthew Dubourg after John Heaviside Clarke, *The Day after Waterloo*, 1816. Musée de l'Armée, Brussels. Photo: Patrick Lorette / The Bridgeman Art Library **p. 40** William Quiller Orchardson, *Napoleon on Board the Bellerophon*, 1906. Anne S. K. Brown Military Collection, Brown University Library **p. 41** Unknown artist, *Napoleon I Dictating His Notes to His Young Assistant on Ile Ste. Helene*. Bibliothèque nationale de France. Photo: Snark / Art Resource, NY **p. 43** Napoleon's Tomb. Les Invalides.

To Marko, with love
  —R. B.

Library of Congress Cataloging-in-Publication Data:

Burleigh, Robert.
Napoleon: the story of the little corporal / by Robert Burleigh.
p. cm.
"Published in association with the American Federation of Arts."
ISBN-13: 978-0-8109-1378-3
ISBN-10: 0-8109-1378-X
1. Napoleon I, Emperor of the French, 1769–1821—Juvenile literature. 2. France—History—1789–1815—Juvenile literature.
3. Emperors—France—Biography—Juvenile literature. I. Title.

DC203.B943 2007
944.05092—dc22
[B]
2006023610

Text copyright © 2007 Robert Burleigh

Book design by Celina Carvalho

Published in 2007 by Abrams Books for Young Readers
An imprint of Harry N. Abrams, Inc.
Printed and bound in China
10 9 8 7 6 5 4 3 2 1

HNA ■■■■■
harry n. abrams, inc.
a subsidiary of La Martinière Groupe
115 West 18th Street
New York, NY 10011
www.hnabooks.com